TRAVELING ACROSS

NORTH AMERICA

1812—1813

PAVEL SVININ
Engraving by an
unknown artist

TRAVELING ACROSS

NORTH AMERICA

1812—1813

WATERCOLORS
BY THE RUSSIAN DIPLOMAT
PAVEL SVININ

*Sixty-eight watercolors
from the collection of
the Russian Museum,
St. Petersburg*

HARRY N. ABRAMS, INC., PUBLISHERS, NEW YORK
IZOKOMBINAT "KHUDOZHNIK RSFSR", ST. PETERSBURG

Editor: Nora Beeson

Designer: Yevgeny Bolshakov

Translated from the Russian by Kathleen Carroll

English text edited by: Yuri Pamfilov

Project Manager: Yuri Ilyin

LIBRARY OF CONGRESS CATALOGING-IN-PUBLICATION DATA

Svinin, Pavel Petrovich, 1788—1839.
Traveling across North America 1812—1813:
watercolors by the Russian diplomat/Pavel Svinin;
Translated from the Russian by Kathleen Carroll
p. 192   20.5×16.5 cm
ISBN 0-8109-3855-3
1. United States — Description and travel — 1783—1848.
2. Canada — Description and travel — 1783—1867.
3. United States — Description and travel — 1783—1848 — Views.
4. Canada — Description and travel — 1783—1867 — Views.
5. Svinin, Pavel Petrovich, 1788—1839 — Journeys — North America.
6. Watercolor painting, Russian.
7. Watercolor painting — 19th century — Russian S.F.S.R.
8. Russians — Travel — United States — History — 19th centry. I. Title.
E 165.S987 1992
917.304'5—dc20   91—23944
CIP

Contents

INTRODUCTION

In November 1817, Pyotr Volkonsky, then Minister of the Imperial Court, addressed the following inquiry to the General Staff on behalf of Emperor Alexander I: "It would please His Majesty the Emperor that you find out whether the Hermitage library or print collection contain various views of North and South American cities and their environs... and if such are found, then His Majesty would like them to be delivered immediately to Moscow...." [1]

At the same time a similar letter was sent to the Russian embassies in England and America. [2]

It seems that the Russian ambassadors were unable to satisfy the Emperor's sudden interest in views of America. As Khristofor Lieven reported from London in March 1818: "I did my best to locate the color views of the cities of North and South America, and of their environs, in local bookstores and print shops. With great regret I must inform Your Excellency that the number of prints which I could find here is extremely limited and the quality of most of them is less than adequate...." [3]

A similar reply was sent in 1818 from Philadelphia by the Russian envoy Andrei Dashkov, who emphasized that "such works of art are scarce in America." [4]

Evidently representations of America were a great rarity not only in Russia at the beginning of the nineteenth century. Judging by various publications kept in Moscow and St. Petersburg libraries, even in the United States itself there were not many views of America painted at the turn of the nineteenth century. All the more interesting, therefore, are the pictures made by Pavel Svinin during his journeys across North America between 1811 and 1813. More than sixty years ago a book came out in New York in which fifty-two works were reproduced from Svinin's portfolio belonging at that time to R. T. H. Halsey. He had acquired the portfolio in America from a fellow countryman who had worked in post-revolutionary Russia as a Red Cross representative. [5]

In the preface to this edition, Halsey writes how all those interested in the subject gradually became fascinated with the work and personality of the artist. As a result, the original idea of reproducing three views of New York, in *Iconography of Manhattan Island*, grew into a special edition, with two articles, published in 1930. The first article was contributed by Halsey, the owner of the portfolio, and the second by Avrahm Yarmolinsky, who then headed the Slavic Division of the New York Public Library, and who had devoted much effort to tracing Svinin's biography.

After traveling to Russia, and locating books published by Svinin, Yarmolinsky was the first to provide a profile of the author of the views of America. It goes without saying that Yarmolinsky also came into contact with museum specialists attempting to discover the artist's original drawings and watercolors, but he was told that these works had disappeared about a century earlier. This was really the case, although, besides the fifty-two subjects published in 1930 by Halsey and Yarmolinsky, two albums of Svinin's watercolors with views of America were transferred in 1953 from the Soviet Ministry of Culture to the Russian Museum in Leningrad. Seventeen of these are identical to those owned by Halsey in 1930, but more than fifty have no counterparts among the subjects reproduced in 1930 in New York.

Until quite recently the author of this article had no idea of the whereabouts of the watercolors once owned by Halsey. At present, thanks to Edward Kasinec, head of the Slavic Division of the New York Public Library, they have been located in the Metropolitan Museum of Art.

For the time being we are absolutely certain that besides those published in 1930 in New York there exist an additional sixty-eight watercolors with views of America executed by Svinin between 1811 and 1813. The watercolors from the Russian Museum in St. Petersburg reproduced here show an America without skyscrapers, an America during the difficult romantic period of its history.

Unfortunately, many of the pictures are impossible to decipher. One would need to be an expert in American architecture to reliably identify this or that view. Therefore we will leave to our American colleagues the task of determining which cities and which buildings are portrayed by Svinin. We will merely note that the cities of New York, Washington, and others, judging by the extant St. Paul's Cathedral or City Hall, located in New York, are fully recognizable in the works of the Russian artist.

In the beginning of the nineteenth century there were naturally no gigantic skyscrapers in the background, and, instead of asphalt and cars, the newly completed buildings were surrounded by young trees. And Mount Vernon, to which George Washington retired to live, looked different than it does today. The humble earthen hill, depicted by Svinin, was later replaced by the Washington family crypt with its mighty gate of brown brick.

Since much has changed in America over the last two centuries, it is all the more interesting to see this country through the eyes of a Russian artist active in the early nineteenth century.

The watercolors are also noteworthy because they serve as illustrations to two books that Svinin published for a Russian readership which knew extremely little about America. In his *View on the Republic of the United States of America* (St. Petersburg, 1814) and *An Attempt at a Pictorial Account of a Trip Across North America* (St. Petersburg, 1815), Svinin describes in a lively and unconstrained manner all the peculiarities of the country he has seen, sometimes comparing it to England or Russia.

An Attempt at a Pictorial Account begins as follows: "Nature in this part of the New World is striking for its magnificence and beauty. Its original inhabitants and artifacts offer wide opportunities for researchers, while the colonies that comprise it, their way of government, laws, political life, family relations and customs stemming from

ОПЫТЪ

ЖИВОПИСНАГО ПУТЕШЕСТВІЯ

ПО СѢВЕРНОЙ АМЕРИКѢ

Павла Свиньина.

———

И въ самыхъ горестяхъ насъ можетъ
утѣшать
Воспоминаніе минувшихъ дней блажен-
ныхъ!

Элегія Анд. Тургенева.

Продается въ книжныхъ лавкахъ Ивана
Заикина подъ No. 18, 23 и 26.

ВЪ САНКТПЕТЕРБУРГѢ

ВЪ ТИПОГРАФІИ Ф. ДРЕХСЛЕРА.

1815.

TITLE PAGE OF THE BOOK *AN ATTEMPT AT A PICTORIAL ACCOUNT OF A TRIP ACROSS NORTH AMERICA* (In Russian, published in St. Petersburg in 1815).

various peoples of the world, as well as their rapid development in all spheres, represent a phenomenon unprecedented in the history of man." [6] In admiration of America's natural scenery, Svinin notes that "the United States of America, like Russia, encompasses almost all climates from the very coldest to the hottest." [7]

And further: "The rivers which flow within the borders of the United States of America are remarkable for their depth and breadth.... American lakes are the size of oceans.... The forests are the main wealth of this land, both as regards the great variety of trees and the high quality of their wood, and these forests are a lovely spectacle to behold. An artist would hardly find the right colors on his palette to reproduce the shades of their verdure. The most vivid purple and heavenly azure strike one alternately; the incomparable magnolia is seen everywhere, and on a tree the size of a hundred-year-old oak one finds fragrant flowers." [8]

From Svinin's account of this exotic fairy-tale land, the Russian reader learned that the United States had an incredible number of the known species of animals on earth, that its gulfs and rivers abounded in fish, of which thirty varieties were sold at the market, and that in Virginia, in the James River, people even caught sterlet that was hitherto unknown outside Russia. [9]

However, the book contains not only ecstatic descriptions of natural beauty but also acquaints the reader with the history of the formation of the United States, its governmental system and the basic provisions of its constitution. The author cites numerous statistical data and gives his observations on economics, industry, culture, and other areas. Thus, he writes that "according to the last census of

1810, the population of the United Territories was 7,230,514," [10] of which there were some 106,000 free and 1,185,823 enslaved Negroes, [11] and no more than 60,000 Indians. [12]

Speculating upon the military might of the United States, Svinin notes that "it takes years and wars to make soldiers," and, therefore, "the American army is in very poor condition due to its newness, and is especially in need of officers. But as far as the personal courage of Americans is concerned, of this they have no lack." [13]

To support his view, he refers to, the fact that the Americans managed to capture three frigates and two sloops in the war with the British. [14] According to Svinin, in 1813 the Americans had 23 warships, including "10 big frigates, as well as 160 gunboats. Another 10 frigates were being built." [15]

The Russian traveler notes the spirit of enterprise that enables Americans to achieve technical progress. He admires their high level of education and democracy: "The son of the richest banker attends the same school as that of the poorest day laborer. Each learns the geography of his country, knows the fundamentals of arithmetic, and has a general understanding of other sciences." [16]

With certain envy Svinin reports that every city in North America has several newspapers. "In New York alone, 19 different newspapers are published, of which five come out in the morning and just as many in the evening. In Philadelphia and Boston there are just as many." And further: "People of all financial standings read newspapers, for in addition to business activities which are so closely linked to politics, each citizen, having a voice in administration, wishes to know the course of state affairs." [17]

Рис: съ Натуры П: Св.

Часть Нїагарскаго

Водопада.

NIAGARA FALLS

VIEW OF
MORRISVILLE,
GENERAL MOREAU'S
COUNTRY HOUSE
IN PENNSYLVANIA
Drawing from life
by Pavel Svinin.
From the book
*An Attempt at
a Pictorial
Account of a Trip
Across North
America.*

Рис: съ Натуры П: Св...

Морисъ-виль. Усадьба
Генерала Моро въ Америкѣ.

Of course, Svinin tells the readers of the different political parties existing in the United States and of the wide variety of religious beliefs in practice there. Naturally, the author muses over the prospects of mutual relations between America and Russia. In his opinion, trade in hemp, candles, linen, and other goods could develop successfully were his countrymen to observe certain norms and quality. In other words, his books provide a vast wealth of information about a distant and unknown land called America, a land described graphically and true-to-life by an attentive and well-meaning observer.

But it was not by accident that Svinin called his book *An Attempt at a Pictorial Account of a Trip Across North America.* The artist clearly intended to publish it along with his pictures. In the summer of 1816, he submitted the book and two portfolios of drawings [18] to Empress Elizaveta Alexeyevna. On August 4 of that year Svinin received a letter from Nikolai Longinov, secretary to the Empress, which read as follows:

"M(y) d(ear) S(ir)

Pavel Petrovich,

By the highest order of Her Majesty E(mpress) E(lizaveta) A(lexe-yevna), it is my honor to return your portfolio of drawings with views of America and, at the same time, to inform you, M(y) d(ear) S(ir), that Her Majesty's curiosity was satisfied to the fullest and perusal of this collection of pictures afforded her great pleasure."[19]

Thus, Svinin's hopes of high-level financing of his book with engraved views of America did not come true. It was an expensive undertaking, on which the Empress was evidently not willing to take a risk. The author, contrary to standard practice and tradition, for some reason chose not to present the albums to the ruler as a gift. It seems most likely that he still had some hope of publishing them.

It cannot be ruled out that Andrei Dashkov had in mind Svinin's "little pictures" with views of America when he wrote to St. Petersburg in June 1818: "I hope.... to deliver several prints and drawings which cannot be found either in England or Europe and which you may find curious, if not for their artistic value, then at least for their novelty and true-to-life quality."[20] Svinin and Dashkov knew each other well. Svinin may have left behind in Philadelphia the watercolors about which the Russian envoy wrote in his letter to St. Petersburg.

The watercolors reproduced in this book were received by the Russian Museum in 1953. So far it has not been possible to trace their provenance prior to that time. Until now they have not been put to scholarly use and remain, for all intents and purposes, unknown to specialists and art lovers alike.[21]

Nevertheless, these watercolors represent quite a rare collection of landscapes, views, and genre scenes reflecting the artist's direct impressions of America. They are unique not only as interesting iconographic material about the North America of the early nineteenth century, but also in that Svinin, an artist and a diplomat, was not confined by any departmental instructions of how and what to draw, as was usually the case.

Perhaps since Svinin was free to choose his own subjects and means of expression, many of the watercolors from his American albums fully correspond, in style and genre, to the artistic quests of the new century. They are expressive, not varied in color but harmoniously picturesque. These realistic works, devoid of any excessive idealization, reflect the artist's poetic perception of nature and the tenor of American life, which fills them with great lyricism.

The watercolor cycle, created by Svinin, is not the only example of Russian artists recording their travel impressions at that time. By the early nineteenth century, there already existed in Russia the tradition of depicting natural surroundings, native dress, and everyday life of different peoples. Many artists traveled with sketchbook in hand. The famous landscape painter Mikhail Ivanov (1748—1823) produced numerous watercolor views of various Russian cities. Siberia's wonderful scenery and the little-known customs of its inhabitants were depicted by Vasily Petrov (1770—1810), Andrei Martynov (1768—1826), Yemelyan Korneyev (1782?—after 1834), and by other painters as well. These were not just fine professionals educated in the St. Petersburg Academy of Arts; each of them, to varying degrees, advocated the then dominant doctrine of Classicism and fulfilled commissions from official circles.

The watercolors, drawings, and paintings by the early nineteenth-century traveling artists, prompted by their impressions of new places, unusual customs, and appearances of different peoples inhabiting Russia, are incomparably more vivid and emotional than the majority of landscapes of that time. They make up a most interesting and significant chapter in the history of Russian art. And still, Svinin's watercolors stand up well even against the high standards of these works, thanks to their spontaneity, pictorial freedom, and keen observation.

Svinin's nonethnographic approach differed markedly from the manner used by contemporary artists portraying exotic peoples and

OPPOSITE:
INDIANS,
THE NATIVE
INHABITANTS
OF NORTH
AMERICA

Рис: съ Натуры П: Св...

УВЕСЕЛЕНІЯ ИНДѢЙЦЕВЪ,

ПРИРОДНЫХЪ ЖИТЕЛЕЙ СѢВЕР-
НОЙ АМЕРИКИ.

Предоставляя себѣ до другова
времени подробное описаніе Индѣй-
цовъ, сихъ любопытныхъ и мало
извѣстныхъ еще народовъ, пред-
ставляющихъ обширное поле для
догадокъ историка и удивляющихъ
разнообразными противуположно-
стями характера и обычаевъ сво-
ихъ: соединяя лютое звѣрство съ
великодушіемъ, корыстолюбіе съ
безкорыстіемъ, умъ пылкій и про-

customs. His watercolors are indeed travel sketches capturing the spontaneous rhythm of movement and fleeting impressions. His townscapes of New York, Washington, and California are striking for their unostentatious quality and their accurate, albeit rather generalized, depiction of American architecture which already in the early nineteenth century was thrusting skyward.

Among Svinin's watercolors there are quite a number of landscapes. Not views, but real landscapes, each with its own representational framework, be it riverbanks overgrown with thickets (*Riverbanks*), a tangle of tall trees on an island (*View of an Island*), or roads meandering along rivers and around lakes.

The artist's descriptions in his books about America echo many of his watercolors. Thus, Svinin devotes an entire chapter to Niagara Falls, and four watercolors painted from various vantage points provide the viewer with a visual representation of this natural wonder. In the rather small drawings the artist was able to convey the might and power of raging torrents of water as if they had "frozen" for one fraction of a moment under his brush.

Impressed by the rapid growth of technology and characteristic concerns for comfort and convenience in the United States, Svinin, in his *Attempt at a Pictorial Account of a Trip Across North America*, writes at length about steamships, roads, and bridges over rivers. While giving Americans their due for the religious tolerance they display, he deliberately focuses the viewer's attention on the various religions practiced in the United States. Some rituals he describes in detail. Thus, one of his watercolor sketches illustrates the rite of baptism, and another a Methodist worship service, or rather its culmination when the frenzied believers throw themselves on the ground and "let out howls and moans."

Both watercolors are in fact very interesting genre compositions, each with its own story and distinct characterization of the persons portrayed. Of course, Svinin did not draw these scenes from life: inspired by his impressions, he "composed" the pictures, imparting to them a sense of drama.

Svinin's watercolors include many scenes from American everyday life. Uprooting trees (*On the Plantation*), leveling a road, traveling by stagecoach — all these subjects illustrate a peaceful, calm existence. But for the Russian viewer these depictions meant more, as similar "scenes of everyday life" occurred very seldom in contemporary Russian art.

The fact that genre scenes did not appear by accident in Svinin's creative output is confirmed by the pictures reproduced in the 1930 New York edition where many of the scenes demonstrate the artist's interest in concrete life situations and in the minute nuances of human behavior: He depicts people of different character in a stagecoach (fig. 14), in a tavern (fig. 12), on the street (fig. 15), at a parade (fig. 20), and in a park (fig. 21).

Many of the watercolors are unusual for Russian art of the 1810s: some are clearly romantic in spirit (*Rainbow*, *Landscape with Moon*); others not only portray real-life situations, but also reveal the artist's ability to represent them quite expressively and in a genre manner (*Baptism*, *Worship Service of Negro Methodists*). A third group is striking for their simple motifs (*Riverbanks*, *View of an Island*), which the artist elevates to a surprisingly subtle poetic image.

Рис. съ Натуры П: Св...

Ловля трески, на Отмѣли
Новой Земли.

CODFISHING
Drawing from [
by Pavel Svini
From the book
An Attempt
at a Pictorial
Account of a Tr
Across North
America.

Indeed, in the Russia of the turn of the nineteenth century one could hardly acquire such skills and preferences in painting. More likely, Svinin's formation as an artist was influenced by his acquaintance with European art during his stay in England before his trip to America.

Who then was Pavel Svinin? How and when did he arrive in America? Back in 1930, relying on reference material and Svinin's own essays, Avrahm Yarmolinsky gave the American reader a fairly detailed answer to this question. But that was a long time ago. Knowledge of Russia and of her culture has since grown in America. The names of Pushkin and Gogol are now familiar to many Americans. The "Age of Pushkin" in Russian culture has become a common concept not only in Russia. Pavel Svinin belongs to that very same "Pushkin" generation of the Russian intelligentsia, the study of which is extremely important to understanding Russia.

Pavel Petrovich Svinin was a striking, yet very contradictory, figure. As a writer, journalist, diplomat, artist, publisher, and collector, he made more than a modest contribution to Russian culture. During his lifetime he was very famous, but today, unfortunately, he is almost forgotten. His contemporaries are partly to blame for this. Disliking Svinin's bent for fantasies and exaggerations, and his excessive servility, they dedicated caustic epigrams to him. [22]

One might ask "So what of it?" At that time many people became targets for fun-poking and poetic gibes. But Svinin's love of fantasies, combined with his intense public and literary activity, quite often provoked irritation. Xenophont Polevoi (1801—1867), brother of the well-known Russian journalist and writer Nikolai Polevoi (1796—

23

Рис: съ Натуры П:Св...

Стимботъ или паровое
Судно.

STEAMBOAT

Imagine a vessel which looks like a flat-bottomed frigate; imagine that it's not afraid of storms, doesn't need wind, always runs with surprising speed and safety, and completes its course according to schedule; inside it one can enjoy peace, contentment, and even the most whimsical fancies of a luxurious life. There you have a picture of the American steamboat!... This invention has become so useful and convenient that the past seven years have seen 16 steamboats paddling through the waters of the United States....

I imagine with pleasure the good use that would come through introduction of the steamboat in Russia. Just think how many thousands of strong hands would be freed to return to the vast fields formerly cultivated by pooz or decrepit old men, promising a generous requital for their work there. Gaiety, conjugal love, and fidelity would be reestablished in the deserted villages, and instead of the physical exhaustion and often death, which met the peasant pulling barges behind a tow line, he will find true wealth and good health behind the plough. Besides all that, our most precious treasure — our forests, whose wood is used in vast quantities to build barges, will be saved. (pp. 84, 93, 103, 104)

1846), recorded a very interesting episode which clearly illustrates on what grounds conflicts could have arisen for Svinin.

"Once I was at his place [Alexander Pushkin's. — Ye. P.] together with Pavel Petrovich Svinin. Pushkin, as I gathered from our conversation, was angry with Svinin for having very awkwardly and inopportunely introduced him at a ball to a certain Miss L., known for her beauty and social graces. There was no better way to insult Pushkin than to introduce him as the celebrated poet, and Svinin had committed this blunder. For which the poet, as I was witness, paid him back with malice. In addition to reproaching him heatedly and asking him never to take it upon himself to introduce him to anyone in the future, no matter who it was, Pushkin, having regained his composure, then turned the conversation to Svinin's adventures in Bessarabia, where Svinin had been charged with an important mission by the government but had acted in such a way that he had been dismissed from all activities of his office. Pushkin began interrogating him so cleverly and adeptly that the unhappy Svinin twitched as if on pins and needles." [23]

Pushkin took vengeance on Svinin in yet another way, for it was the latter's Bessarabian adventures that served as a basic plot, later passed on to Nikolai Gogol, who used it in his comedy *The Inspector General*. [24] Thus Svinin came to be remembered as a sort of prototype for Khlestakov, the main character in Gogol's famous play. The satirical image created by the great writer, and a few graphic episodes recounted by contemporaries, obscured the true image of Pavel Svinin. The stigma of "Khlestakovism," [25] which became associated with his name, distorted the true picture of his relationship with those around him for the duration of his unusual and extremely full life.

Information about Pavel Svinin is extremely scarce and far from being always correct. According to documents, the basic outline of his biography is as follows:

Svinin was born in 1787, the son of the landowner Pyotr Nikiphorovich Svinin from Galich. [26] He studied at the "Boarding School for the Nobility" attached to Moscow University together with Vasily Zhukovsky and the brothers Alexander and Nikolai Turgenev. At that time he began to write verses which were published in the St. Petersburg magazine *Utrennyaya Zarya* (*Morning Dawn*) in 1804.

Having an interest in drawing, Svinin came to St. Petersburg and entered the Academy of Arts. His study of painting there did not last long, although he preserved his attachment to art for the rest of his life. Later, in 1810, he presented to the Academy two pictures, *Landscape* and *Cossacks Leading Turkish Prisoners* (whereabouts unknown), whose sufficiently high merits were acknowledged when the artist received permission to paint a program work to obtain the title of Academician. In 1811 Svinin was granted this title for his canvas *Suvorov Relaxing by the Stream.* Unfortunately, the whereabouts of this canvas are also unknown. Yet, judging by Svinin's letter to the board of the Academy, the picture apparently exemplified a rare instance of a romantic treatment of a historic subject. "Svinin intended to depict a subject from most recent history that conformed to his own feelings and his favorite technique [possibly the watercolor technique is implied here — Ye. P.)." In order to portray Suvorov relaxing in a simple everyday setting, the artist wished to show him "in the early morning when dawn begins to engulf nature." [27]

Svinin's romantic attitude to the landscape background in this historical painting has unmistakable affinities with his emotional perception of nature in America as manifest in his albums of 1811 to 1813. After being granted the title of Academician, he continued to work in the visual arts throughout his life. He executed an enormous number of pictures with views of Russian cities, which were published as illustrations to his articles in various editions during the 1810s and 1830s. [28]

Svinin's official occupation for many years was his service in the Ministry of Foreign Affairs. On March 13, 1805, [29] he was employed as an archivist of the Moscow Archives, and was immediately sent to manage the correspondence of the State Chancellor Count Alexander Vorontsov, remaining with him until his death in 1806. On June 14 of the same year, Svinin was "promoted to translator" for the State Board of the Ministry of Foreign Affairs. On August 8, 1806, "by Imperial order he was sent to handle foreign correspondence for Vice-Admiral Dmitry Sinyavin, commander of the Russian squadron in the Mediterranean and the Archipelago, and remained in this squadron during the battle at Tenedos Island on March 8, 1807. On the arrival of the squadron in Lisbon, he was sent with dispatches to the Imperial Court on November 10, 1807. [30] For outstanding service during the siege of the Tenedos Fortress, he was awarded the Order of St. Vladimir of the fourth degree, with bow, on March, 4, 1808. [31] In his *Naval Reminiscences* (St. Petersburg, 1818—19), Svinin described his life on board the ship *Raphael* under the command of Sinyavin.

On August 5, 1811, by Imperial order, Svinin was sent to Philadelphia as secretary to the Consul General N. Ya. Kozlov, [32] and served two years in North America.

At that time diplomatic relations between Russia and the United States were just in the making. The question of an exchange of diplomatic representatives had been resolved only in the summer of 1808. On July 1, 1809, Andrei Dashkov arrived in Philadelphia in the capacity of the first Russian Consul. On November 5 of the same year, the American envoy John Quincy Adams [33] officially presented his credentials to Alexander I in St. Petersburg. Russian consulates were opened in three cities of the United States: Philadelphia (July 1, 1809), Boston (August 24, 1809), and Washington (May 29, 1810).

In addition to their usual tasks, Russian diplomats were instructed "to study the traditions and customs of the country of their residence, to encourage active and direct trade, and to develop mutually beneficial relations between both countries." [34] In his activities in America, Pavel Svinin selflessly and persistently pursued these aims.

In 1814, the St. Petersburg journal *Syn Otechestva* (*Son of the Fatherland*) [35] carried chapters from Svinin's books *View on the Republic of the United States of America* [36] and *An Attempt at a Pictorial Account of a Trip Across North America*, [37] which were published in 1814 and 1815.

In the capacity of secretary to the Russian Consul, Svinin collected materials about America, using literature, accounts in the press, and his own observations. All this information is reflected in his books about this country. But he did not confine himself to acquainting Russians with America, and in 1813 he published a book in Philadelphia about Moscow and St. Petersburg with his own illustrations. [38]

In spite of certain inaccuracies, these essays have not lost their significance today. Modern researchers derive information about early nineteenth-century America from Svinin's books. The famous Soviet scholar and expert in American studies, Nikolai Bolkhovitinov, writes: "Factual information and the recommendations of Pavel Svinin were based on his practical experience and were totally substantiated by several other sources, among them archival materials." [39]

In the summer of 1813 Svinin was assigned the important mission of accompanying to Russia the famous General Jean Victor Moreau (1763—1813), a fierce opponent of Napoleon who had been banished from France and was living in the United States. Alexander I had invited General Moreau to Russian service as a man capable of leading the united forces against Napoleon. After a warm meeting with the Emperor in Prague, the general set off for the army in the field.

An entry in the diary of Pavel Pushchin, a Russian army officer, dated August 3, 1813, reads as follows: "General Moreau, having recently arrived from America, overtook us today in the field. He was in civilian dress and riding in a carriage headed for St. Petersburg along with Svinin, whom I knew well." [40]

According to Svinin's own account, he remained at the general's side up to his death near Dresden, where in the very first battle Moreau had his right leg torn off and his left leg badly maimed. Moreau died in September 1813, and his body was transported to St. Petersburg and buried in the Church of St. Catherine on Nevsky Prospekt.

On September 9, 1813, Svinin, who personally knew Moreau's family, was sent, by Imperial order, to London with a letter and an

WORSHIP SERVICE OF NEGRO METHODISTS Drawing from life by Pavel Svinin. From the book *An Attempt at a Pictorial Account of a Trip Across North America.*

30

Рис: съ Натуры П: Св...

Богослуженiе Африканскихъ.
Методистовъ.

allowance for the general's widow. According to his certificate of service, on December 26, 1813, he was sent with dispatches from London to the General Staff; on March 20, 1814, he was again dispatched to London as courier; and finally, on June 21 of that year, he was sent from London with dispatches to Russia. [41]

Thus fate brought Svinin and General Moreau together.

A reporter by nature, Svinin recorded everything he saw and experienced in a book about Moreau. In his preface to the Russian edition, which, however, was never published, he wrote: "During my stay in London after the death of General Moreau, unfounded rumors and the desire of his widow, the Prince Regent, and the public in general to have a description of... the last minutes... of this famous hero, compelled me to put in order the daily records of our trip from America and to publish them in French, attaching thereto a short biography of his life. Its success surpassed all expectations. My book was received with extraordinary attention and approval in England. In a very short time it was reprinted twice in French and English, and also immediately translated into German and Spanish. The English government itself bought 500 copies for secret use, and soon I learned that it had been reprinted in Geneva, Paris, and Philadelphia as well." [42]

In Russia, Svinin's book about Moreau never came out in a separate edition; however, a chapter devoted to him was included in *An Attempt at a Pictorial Account of a Trip Across North America*. The chapter opens with an engraving showing the view of General Moreau's estate, which Svinin describes in this way: "The village of Morrisville lies at the foot of the rapids of the Delaware River some 50 miles from New York and 30 from Philadelphia." The engraving depicts a house with a portico and four columns. Several watercolors from Svinin's album also present this view.

Subsequently Svinin's life proceeded as follows: on June 15, 1815, he was sent to Bessarabia for a review of that area and description of its administration. [43] Judging by Svinin's own notes, he was given secret instructions, wherein he had "the right to hear the complaints of Bessarabian citizens and, investigating them on the spot, to report...his opinion" [44] to the Committee of Ministers.

Apparently this circumstance was unknown to Alexander Pushkin, who considered Svinin to have exceeded his authority by actively interfering in the lives of the inhabitants. However, Pushkin may not have been the only one who thought that way, for Svinin did indeed suffer some kind of a setback in Bessarabia. Later, in the 1820s, he attempted to explain the reasons for his "ill success," [45] but the notes that have survived are too fragmentary and do not disclose the heart of the matter.

Having returned from Bessarabia, Svinin continued to serve in the Ministry of Foreign Affairs, moving up in rank and receiving the titles of Collegiate Councillor (1823), Honorable Member of the Armory, and Councillor of State (1824). Nevertheless, in June 1824 Svinin submitted a request for his resignation "on account of poor health." [46]

It is difficult to judge the true condition of Svinin's health at that time. But retirement was necessary for him to engage in literary and journalistic endeavors. Beginning in 1818 he was occupied with the publication of *Otechestvennye zapiski* (*Notes of the Fatherland*), [47] one of the most popular magazines at that time. He traveled extensively around Russia, writing numerous feature stories about the history, nature, everyday life, and morals of different peoples. Travel impressions, discourses about economics, customs, literary profiles of talented people, such as the inventor Ivan Kulibin, who was discovered by Svinin, made up the bulk of his writings. Later, after Svinin's death, these scattered essays were put together in the book *Pictures of Russia and the Everyday Life of Its Peoples* (St. Petersburg, 1839), which was splendidly illustrated by the author himself.

Besides journalism, Svinin was consumed by other passions as well. One of the most important among them was his love for Russian history and art. Not only did he stubbornly continue to paint, sketch, and make lithographic prints, he, in fact, became one of the first chroniclers of the history of Russian art of the 1820s and 1830s. His comprehensive reviews of exhibits at the Academy of Arts, published in the *Notes of the Fatherland*, reflect the way in which critical thought was developing in Russia. Svinin's articles vividly convey his contemporaries' perception of the work of Kiprensky, Venetsianov, the young Alexander Ivanov and Karl Briullov, and many other lesser-known Russian painters.

Svinin's love of art became manifest in yet another field of his activity, extremely important in its conception, but never completely realized. Apparently he wrote the anonymous "Proposal for the Institution of a Russian National Museum," published in the magazine *Son of the Fatherland* (1817, No. 13). The idea of the creation of such a museum was prompted by a growth of national consciousness following the war with Napoleon and the fact that there were many talented artists and remarkable private collections in Russia at that time. This idea was literally "hanging in the air," but it was first clearly formulated in the above-mentioned article. Its author wrote: "Countless historical and artistic monuments are scattered throughout the state in the hands of private individuals, who often have no idea of their value, and, furthermore, a significant part of their value is lost because they exist singly and unrelated to one another, while it is only through this relation that they could be elucidated and explained properly. Moreover, they are subject to accidental damage and even annihilation, and most of them will be lost for history." [48]

In anticipation of a state decision regarding the creation of a Russian museum, Svinin, using his own funds, put together a splendid collection. His paintings, sculptures, ancient manuscripts, coins, miniatures, silverware, and books comprised a genuine museum providing an insight into the history and development of Russian culture. His collection included paintings by Losenko, Kiprensky, Venetsianov, Briullov, Tropinin, and other outstanding masters of the Russian school.

In 1834, in financial ruin, Svinin was forced to sell his collection at auction [49] Before taking this extreme step, he appealed to the Russian government with the following proposal set forth in a letter to Pyotr Volkonsky, Minister of the Imperial Court: "During 12 years of travel around Russia," wrote Svinin on February 6, 1834, "I had the opportunity to amass a collection of Russian works in many areas of science and the arts.... The circumstances of my having to leave the capital and move to the country deprive me of the possibility to keep my collection any longer. I have decided to sell it, and one merchant from London who conducts extensive trade in art has made me an offer to acquire my museum for 110,000 rubles.... Since my collection contains many Russian objects of great rarity, I would not consider their sale outside the country without the assent of His Majesty the Emperor. Perhaps it will be the desire of His Imperial Majesty to order these things to remain in Russia? In such case I, for my part, am prepared to make necessary sacrifices: For my main goal in creating this museum is to lay the cornerstone to the founding of a National Museum so necessary for Russia." [50]

Svinin's noble gesture was not supported by Nicholas I. The Emperor's decision is handwritten in a letter: "I grant permission to sell abroad." Judging by Svinin's further correspondence with the Imperial Court, a portion of the collection was bought by Baron Alexander von Humboldt. [51] The rest was scattered among private collections in Russia.

As a unique monument of Russian culture, Svinin's collection ceased to exist in the mid-1830s. But its composition can be restored, though perhaps only partially, thanks to the catalog [52] that he published and to an album of watercolors (Tretyakov Gallery, Moscow), in which the pictures belonging to him were carefully sketched.

The collection contained such remarkable canvases as *Jupiter and Thetis* and *Portrait of the Actor Volkov* by Losenko, *Portrait of Alexander Khrapovitsky* by Levitsky, *The Lace Maker* by Tropinin, and other paintings which now hang in the Russian Museum and the Tretyakov Gallery.

Thus, to a certain degree, Svinin's dream came true, although his idea of the creation of a state collection of Russian art accessible to the public was realized only half a century later, at the very end of the nineteenth century, when the Russian Museum was opened.

Svinin's other interests were literature and history. He himself wrote plays, poetry, and novels. Of course, one would hardly rank him among the most talented writers and poets who brought fame to Russia, but he was one of the many typical representatives of the newly born Russian intelligentsia, which contributed to the development of Russian culture.

Svinin's historical studies, devoted to Peter the Great and Yemelyan Pugachev, were quite fruitful. Pushkin, by the way, used Svinin's account of the defense of the Yaik fortress [53] in his *Captain's Daughter*.[54] Alexander Khrapovitsky's writings, published in the *Notes of the Fatherland* (1821—28), were also widely read by contemporaries.

In 1833 Pavel Svinin became a member of the Russian Academy. In February 1839, having ruined himself by publishing the *Notes of the Fatherland* and augmenting his collections, he could no longer manage his affairs and died in dire poverty in St. Petersburg.

Yevgenia Petrova

ВВЕДЕНІЕ.

———

**Имѣвъ случай провесть два го-
да въ Соединенныхъ Американскихъ
Областяхъ, я обращалъ особенное
вниманіе на изученіе земли сей.**

Натура въ сей части Новаго
Свѣта поражаетъ своимъ величіемъ и чудесностію; природные жители ея и находимыя въ ней древности открываютъ обширное поприще для изслѣдованій и изысканій, а составленіе колоній ея, духъ
правленія ихъ, законы, политическое существованіе, семейственныя
картины, обычаи, происшедшіе отъ

I

I had the chance to spend
two years in the United States,
and I gave special attention
to the study of this land.

LANDSCAPE WITH BUILDINGS

1

RAPIDS

2

The water droplets, flying off from the falling river and carried far in different directions by the wind, coat all surrounding objects with a white layer of sparkling crystals, which gives them strange and eerie shapes.

In some places, huge Gothic buildings loom, in others stand colossal pyramids, splendid columns, ruins, and the like....

The road to this waterfall leads through dense forests and is improved each year. A rather nice hotel for travelers has been built some four versts from it. (One verst equals 3,500 feet; pp. 158, 161, 163, 164, 167, 168, 172)

RAINBOW

3

LANDSCAPE WITH BRIDGE

4

LANDSCAPE WITH FISHERMEN

5

ESTATE

6

LANDSCAPE WITH MOON

7

MANSION IN A PARK

8

LEVELING A ROAD

9

Roads in the United States are repaired yearly and in great haste. Last year there were 37,000 miles of mail routes, of which around 10,000 were impassable. (p. 30)

VIEW OF A SETTLEMENT

10

IN THE FOREST

11

ON THE PLANTATION

12

The surface of its land [America's — Ye. P.] can be deemed more flat than mountainous. It covers 520,000,000 desyatinas (2.7 acres) of rich soil ready to reward generously even the smallest of labors; about 40,000,000 desyatinas of mountainous and wooded land, and 29,000,000 desyatinas of sandy land, not suitable for cultivation. Of the 250,000,000 desyatinas suitable for cultivation, only 40,000,000 were being worked in 1813. (An Attempt at a Pictorial Account of a Trip Across North America, pp. 12, 13)

IN A RUINED MANSION

13

MEETING OF TWO BOATS

14

I was among the viewers during an experiment performed on the *Hudson River involving a new steamboat called the* Paragon. *Carrying 300 tons of cargo, and going against the fast current into a strong head wind, it clocked five* versts *an hour; and going with the stream and with the aid of sail, which it has in case of fair wind, it went a little more than twice as fast...The incredible speed, comfort, and novelty of the steamboat have made it the most often used and favorite means of travel in America, and so, in the summer, mail carriages have been almost completely discontinued between Albany, New York, and Philadelphia. Instead, steamboats go back and forth three times a week, transporting goods and passengers from all points located on their routes, and each time there are no less than 100 travellers on board.* (An Attempt at a Pictorial Account of a Trip Across North America, pp. 98, 99)

CITY ON A RIVER

15

VIEW OF A RIVER

16

VIEW OF A CITY ON A RIVERBANK

17

CITY ON A RIVERBANK

18

WORK ON A RIVERBANK

19

Mechanical inventions have completely replaced human hands in the United States. There everything is done by machine.

RIVERBANKS

20

BRIDGE ACROSS A RIVER

21

VIEW OF A CITY ON A RIVER

22

FORT ON A RIVER

23

BUILDING WITH A TOWER

24

VIEW OF A CITY FROM A RIVER

25

LANDSCAPE WITH RIVER

26

VIEW OF A CITY

27

VIEW OF ROCKY RIVERBANKS

28

VIEW OF A RIVER IN THE MOUNTAINS

29

FORT

30

VILLAGE BY A RIVER

31

LANDSCAPE WITH RIVER

32

LANDSCAPE WITH A ROAD ALONG
A RIVERBANK

33

LANDSCAPE WITH ROAD

34

VIEW OF A VILLAGE ON A RIVERBANK

35

TOWN ON A RIVER

36

LANDSCAPE WITH RIVER

37

OBVERSE AND REVERSE OF A MEDAL
IN HONOR OF GEORGE WASHINGTON

38

MOUNTAIN ROAD

39

VIEW OF AN ISLAND WITH TALL TREES

40

PORTRAIT OF GEORGE WASHINGTON

41

A man well endowed with military talents and high virtues, the immortal Washington. Having given his people peace and freedom following eight years of war, he prescribed peaceful laws for them, and set about being their implementor. (p. 8)

PORTRAIT OF GENERAL MOREAU

42

Europe knows of the great gifts of General Moreau, but not many know of his open and noble character, his pleasant and sincere manner, and other excellent qualities which led everyone who observed him in the family circle into thinking that he had devoted his entire life solely to the discharge of his family obligations...Everyone who saw him was struck by the combination of extreme simplicity and extreme greatness. (An Attempt at a Pictorial Account of a Trip Across North America, p. 111)

WASHINGTON'S TOMB AT MOUNT VERNON

43

VIEW OF WASHINGTON

44

Washington or the federal city was founded in 1792. In 1800, the Congress held its first session there.

The selection of the site for building the national capital was entrusted to George Washington, who, after close scrutiny, considered this place to be the most convenient for the purpose. His choice was based on two main reasons: Firstly, the site is in the very center of the state. And secondly, being located 280 miles from the mouth of the Potomac River, on which it lies (and which, in terms of width and depth is navigable in its entirety), it is a splendid port, and with its domestic connections by means of the river it enjoys all the advantages of domestic trade...The city map encompasses some 14 miles. Streets crisscross in straight lines and are about 90 to 100 feet in width.... The city for the most part exists mainly on paper, for up to the present only Pennsylvania Avenue and a certain portion of Georgetown have been completely built up. Other houses stand so widely apart that one would need to drive over a verst to see one's nearest neighbor.

The Capitol is built on the highest point, which, fortunately, turned out to be in the middle of the city. From there a splendid vista opens up in all directions. (View on the Republic of the United States of America, St. Petersburg, 1814, pp. 49—51)

THE PENNSYLVANIA ACADEMY OF FINE ARTS
(THE FIRST ART SCHOOL IN AMERICA)

45

VIEW OF A VILLAGE FROM A RIVER

46

NEW TALL BUILDING IN NEW YORK

47

The City Hall, completed last year, 1813, is in truth a most splendid building, which could serve as an ornament to any of the leading capitals of Europe. This house is built of white stone, very much like marble, with surprising neatness and finish. It cost over 500,000 dollars to build (View on the Republic of the United States of America, St. Petersburg, 1814, p. 60)

RIVER WITH RAPIDS

48

ST. PAUL'S CATHEDRAL IN NEW YORK

49

50

By the beauty of its buildings and spaciousness, this city is considered to rank first in the United States after Philadelphia, but probably in the near future it will surpass Philadelphia in this respect as well; by the beauty of its location, it has an incomparable advantage over Philadelphia.

The flourishing of New York, as distinct from all other cities, is due primarily to its harbor (a 100-gun ship can throw anchor along the shores and be totally secure from all winds) and to its nearness to the sea, from which it lies a mere 10 versts. These advantages continually attract energetic people and capitalists, for not only does external trade in this port offer a wide field for activity, but domestic trade is in no way inferior to it. The Hudson, or Northern, River that flows through vast tracts of rich and populated land, being a receptacle for many navigable rivers and reaching Canada, has incalculable potential resources and successfully keeps busy a great number of tradesmen...These advantages account for the incredible growth in the population of the city. Thirty years ago there were no more than 10,000 residents here, and now their number has increased tenfold. The city of New York is built on an island. Its first settlers and *founders came in 1614 from Holland, and they bought these rights from the English Captain Hudson, who discovered the mouth of this river, and it was named New Amsterdam.*

The harbor is fortified with heavy guns in the narrow strait on the sea side named Sandy-Hook, which are evidently adequate to thwart encroachment by the largest of enemy fleets. In addition, three-tiered stone batteries have been built on Staten and Governor's Islands, which lie in the middle of the harbor, and there are two more of the same kind at the entrance to the city. (View on the Republic of the United States of America, St. Petersburg, 1814, pp. 57, 58)

NIAGARA FALLS BY MOONLIGHT

51

Being amazed and dumbfounded by the grandeur of the sight, before which I myself seemed but a weak particle, my first thought rises up to the wise creator of this wonder, and with reverence I kiss the hand of the Almighty!

How can I describe all that I felt, all that I saw? The brush of a most skilled painter can recreate an exquisite picture of the beauty he has seen, but can it convey this turbulence, this chaos, this harmony? Looking at this bright crystal wall which seems to be static, suspended in the air, it's hard to believe that this is the same indomitable river which flows with such force and ferocity up above through thousands of granite cliffs, or the one which swirls and boils with a crash in this bottomless infinity!

The incessant roar, which numbs the ears, like the howl of a terrible storm or a destructive crash, drives not only the birds out of the surrounding area, but all predatory animals as well, as it stuns all the senses and organs of sensation.

A foaming column more than 2,000 feet tall rises out of the abyss. And then from it spring black thunderclouds which float continuously above the horizon....

In order to enjoy this incomparably fascinating spectacle to the fullest, one must view this waterfall at sunset, when it appears completely engulfed in flame, and its spray looks like tiny sparks of fire, or at sunrise, when it is adorned with multicolored rainbows, or on a moonlit night amidst the shadows of granite cliffs!

NIAGARA FALLS FROM THE CANADIAN SIDE

52

WATERFALL

53

NIAGARA FALLS

54

REMAINS OF A BEAVER DAM NEAR KENNEBER

_____

55

INDIANS IN A BOAT

56

NEW BRIDGE NEAR PHILADELPHIA

57

The bridges in this land deserve the special attention of any European. Many of them are truly splendid, like the Philadelphia, Trenton, Washington, and Boston Bridges and others as well. But, in terms of structure, the most remarkable and surprising of them all is the bridge built in 1811 across the Schuylkill River near Philadelphia. It is made entirely of wood and consists of a single arch 340 feet in length. (p. 31)

LANDSCAPE IN THE VICINITY
OF PHILADELPHIA

58

VIEW OF MORRISVILLE, GENERAL MOREAU'S
COUNTRY HOUSE IN PENNSYLVANIA

59

60

Methodists and Quakers are essentially among the most predominant religious sects in the United States. They differ one from the other... in their manner of worship and in their dogmas....

New York is the cradle of the Methodist sect in North America. It was founded in 1766 by Philip Embury, an Irish preacher. This sect spread throughout America with incredible rapidity. The greater part of the Negroes living here are the most ardent confessors of this faith. Compelled by curiosity and the stories I'd heard of the peculiar nature and spirit of their worship service, I decided, during my stay in Philadelphia, to visit the African Methodist church along with a friend of mine, and thus came to witness the following.

We entered a large hall or temple, very poorly lit with torches. The smoky blackness of the walls, broken benches, and shattered windows made us instantly uneasy. We advanced almost to the very pulpit and sat down on the third pew. The hall was full of Negroes; the men were gathered on the right side and the women on the left. The dim light of the fire and the frightening faces of the Africans whose eyes, fixed on us, flickered like so many tiny sparks — all this aroused in us a sense of horror, which was further intensified when they began to howl in wild *and shrill voices. It seemed to me that I had fallen into the realm of Pluto among all the frights of hell, and secretly I began to repent for my curiosity, when the doorkeeper, looking very much like Cerberus, locked the door, so no one could leave.*

A black terrifying skeleton stood up in the pulpit and read psalms from the Holy Scripture. At the end of each psalm all the men and women began to sing monotonous verses in loud and piercing voices. This continued for about a half-hour. When the preacher stopped reading, everyone turned to the doors, fell on their knees, bowed their heads to the ground, and began to howl and moan in doleful, heartrending tones. Afterward, the clergyman continued to read the Psalter and, having finished the reading, sat down in a chair; instantly everyone stood up and started singing all together, first the men, then the women, in turns; this lasted about 20 minutes. And then they fell into a silence so deep, so terrifying the like of which usually comes before a storm, when everything goes numb, and the heart quakes in anticipation of something terrible, something inexplicable.

The head preacher began his teaching in a hoarse voice, describing in graphic terms all the horrors of hell and the wrath of God. At first everything went fairly calmly, but little by little the preacher caught fire and ignited the imagination of the listeners with his terrible images and body movements. Then the groaning of the repentant could be heard on all sides, along with the cries and exclamations of those raving as if possessed. Finally, he spoke in a strikingly solemn voice of the destruction of the Universe, pointed to a black cloud fraught with all-destructive thunder, and described all the trials and suffering awaiting sinners: And then the temple shook right down to its very foundation and the arched ceiling rocked from their terrible roar. I must confess that at that moment I too feared real destruction, if not of the Universe, then at least of the choir under which I was sitting and which shook threateningly with each strike of the agonized demon-possessed, who jumped and threw themselves about in all directions and who fell to the ground beating it with their arms and legs, and gnashed their teeth to show that the evil spirits were leaving them. Often in Philadelphia, in the summer, the Methodists gather out of doors and, from a narrow alleyway, direct their prayers toward heaven, which is depicted in this picture. (pp. 46—47)

VIEW OF RICHMOND

61

HAMILTON'S OBELISK AT WEEHAWKEN

62

BAPTISM

63

The Anabaptists, followers of John the Baptist, are baptized in rivers and only after the age of 30. The rite is performed on the first Monday of every month, the weather notwithstanding. During the winter in the northern provinces they make a hole in the ice for this purpose...In Philadelphia I managed to view this magnificent rite. One can neither help feeling a sort of reverence nor resist turning one's thoughts to the River Jordan at the sight of a crowd of people singing in harmony, with hair loose about the shoulders, in dark garments and barefoot, solemnly led by a clergyman to be baptized in the fast river. To add to the splendor and grandeur of this spectacle, claps of thunder and flashes of lightning continued throughout the rite. (pp. 76—79)

AMERICAN STAGECOACH

64

Cities maintain constant contact with one another with the help of public coaches, the number of which varies depending on their trade relations. For example, six such coaches run from Philadelphia to New York daily. They all depart at different hours of the day. (pp. 30, 31)

CODFISHING

65

The *Newfoundland Bank, so famous for its cod catch, is considered to be the richest in the whole world. Its coordinates are 51
degrees west latitude and 50 degrees longitude. Measured with a
straight line, its distance is over 5,000* versts *from St. Petersburg, and
some 700* versts *from the American mainland at the closest point.
On September 29 (Old Style), 1811, on the 24th day of happy sailing,
we reached this bank from Kronstadt....
The morning was unusually fine, not a single cloud covered the sun, a
mild wind gently ruffled the sea and flapped our sails a bit. We breath-
ed the cleanest, lightest air. In three hours we had caught 200 fish;
some of them weighed as much as 45 pounds, and only six or seven
weighed around 10 pounds. No sooner had we cast the lines than we
reeled in our catch, sometimes two fish at once....
Meanwhile, while we were occupied with fishing, huge whales swam
noisily around our ship and amused us with their cheerful rainbow
fountains, which they spouted high into the air through their nostrils.
It seemed that they intended to battle with us and thus to avenge the
ravaging of their kingdom, and they came so near to the ship that
we could see their terrifying jaws.* (pp. 205, 207, 208, 210, 211)

INDIAN ANTIQUITIES

66

What a field for research is presented by North America and its native inhabitants. In its forested interior evidence is continually being discovered that this land was populated by enlightened inhabitants who were familiar with the arts. In recent times, a military camp, or perhaps even a fortress, was discovered near the Ohio River. The choice of location and embankment show that its builders had a knowledge of military arts, while the vases and other objects found in its catacombs testify that they were familiar with other arts as well. These newest discoveries lend themselves more and more to the supposition that the Phoenicians knew about America. (View on the Republic of the United States of America, St. Petersburg, 1814, pp. 30, 31).

MORAVIAN SISTERS

67

CITY STREET

68

ВВЕДЕНIЕ.

Имѣвъ случай провесть два года въ Соединенныхъ Американскихъ Областяхъ, я обращалъ особенное вниманіе на изученіе земли сей.

Натура въ сей части Новаго Свѣта поражаетъ своимъ величіемъ и чудесностію; природные жители ея и находимыя въ ней древности открываютъ обширное поприще для изслѣдованій и изысканій, а составленіе колоній ея, духъ правленія ихъ, законы, политическое существованіе, семейственные картины, обычаи, происшедшіе отъ

THE FIRST PAGE OF P. SVININ'S BOOK

Nature in this part of
the New World is striking in
its majesty and splendor.

NOTES

[1] TsGIA (Central State Historical Archives), fund 0519, inv. 1, 1817, file 380, f. 2

[2] *Ibid, f. 3*

[3] *Ibid, f. 4*

[4] *Ibid, f. 5*

[5] *Picturesque United States of America 1811, 1812, 1813, being A Memoir on Paul Svinin, Russian diplomatic officer, artist and author, containing copious excerpts from his account of his travels in America, with Fifty-Two Reproductions of Water Colors in His Own Sketch-book.* By Avrahm Yarmolinsky, Introduction by R. T. H. Halsey, New York, William Edwin Rudge, 1930

[6] P. P. Svinin, *An Attempt at a Pictorial Account of a Trip Across North America,* St. Petersburg, 1815, p. 1

[7] *Ibid*, p. 13

[8] *Ibid*, pp. 15-19

[9] *Ibid*, pp. 17, 18

[10] *Ibid*, p. 19

[11] *Ibid*, p. 21

[12] *Ibid*, p. 22

[13] *Ibid*, p. 25

[14] *Ibid*

[15] *Ibid*

[16] *Ibid*, p. 33

[17] *Ibid*, pp. 34, 35

[18] TsGIA, fund 535, inv, I, 1816, file 6, ff. 219, 220; ff. 279, 280

[19] *Ibid*, f. 281

[20] *Ibid*, fund 519, inv. I, file 380, f. 7

[21] Five of these works were reproduced in the widely circulated essay about Svinin included in V. P. Vladimirov's book, *New Journeys: Far and Near*, Moscow, 1967.

[22] Perhaps the earliest satire on Svinin belongs to Pyotr Vyazemsky, written after the publication of Svinin's article "A Trip to Gruzino" in *Son of the Fatherland* (1818, part 19, Nos. 39, 40). Vyazemsky reacted negatively to Svinin's panegyric description of Alexei Arakcheyev's estate, located in the town of Gruzino near Novgorod.
Alexander Izmailov's fable *The Liar* (1823) is likewise devoted to the servility and exaggerations noted by contemporaries in Svinin's character and actions, and in his articles with boundless praise for talented, self-taught individuals.

In 1830 Alexander Pushkin portrayed Svinin in his short children's tale, *The Little Liar.* Making a parody of Svinin's passion to fantasize, Pushkin described him as follows: "Pavlusha was a tidy, kind and diligent boy, who had but one vice—he couldn't say three words without lying.

On his name-day his father gave him a little wooden horse. Pavlusha assured everybody that this horse had belonged to Charles XII and was the very same one on which the king had run away from the Battle of Poltava.

Pavlusha maintained that in his parents' home there were a kitchenboy-astronomer and a postilion-historian, and that their poultryman Proshka wrote better verses than Lomonosov. At first all his comrades believed him, but soon they realized he was a liar, and no one believed him anymore, even when he happened to tell the truth." (A. S. Pushkin, *Complete Works*, Moscow, 1949, v. 11, p. 101).

23 *Notes of Xenophont Alexeyevich Polevoi,* St. Petersburg, 1888, p. 276

24 N. V. Gogol, *Complete Works*, Moscow, 1951, v. 4, pp. 524, 525

25 The word derived from the surname Khlestakov, the main character from Gogol's *The Inspector General.* This image became a synonym for boasters and cheats.

26 Galich, an old Russian town in Kostroma province, was founded in the twelfth century. In the early twentieth century there still remained not far from Galich the village of Svinino and the Svinin Hills, named after the local landowners.

27 P. N. Petrov, *A Collection of Materials on the 100-Year-Old History of the St. Petersburg Academy of Arts*, St. Petersburg, 1864, v. 1, p. 552

28 *The Sights of St. Petersburg and Its Environs,* St. Petersburg, 1818—23, with 32 views; *Pictures of Russia and the Everyday Life of Its Peoples*, St. Petersburg, 1839, with numerous "little pictures."

29 Manuscript Department, the State Public Library, fund 679, file 9, f. 1

30 *Ibid*

31 *Ibid*

32 N. N. Bolkhovitinov, *The Development of Russian-American Relations. 1775—1815,* Moscow, 1966, p. 433

33 *Ibid*, p. 364

34 *Ibid*, pp. 350, 351

35 A historical, political, and literary journal published in St. Petersburg from 1812 to 1852 and from 1856 to 1861.

36 *Son of the Fatherland,* 1814, Nos. 45—48.

37 "Observations of a Russian," *Son of the Fatherland,* 1814, Nos. 36—37, p. 386

38 P. Svinin, *Sketches of Moscow and St. Petersburg*, Philadelphia, 1813

39 Bolkhovitinov, *op. cit*, p. 386

40 *Pavel Pushchin's Diary: 1812—1814*, Leningrad, 1987, p. 117

41 Manuscript Department, the State Public Library, fund 679, file 9, f. 1v

42 *Ibid*, file 20, f. 1. ("To the Reader." Preface to the *Life-story of General Moreau*. Manuscript). The following books were published in English by Svinin about Moreau:
Some Details Concerning General Moreau and His Last Moments. Followed by a Short Biographical Sketch by Paul Svinine, Baltimore, E. J. Coale and Harrod and Buel, 1814.
Some Details Concerning General Moreau and His Last Moments. Followed by a Short Biographical Memoir. Second American from the London edition. To which is added a Funeral Oration, pronounced at St. Petersburg, in honor of General Moreau. Translated from the French, Boston, Rowe and Hooper, 1814

43 *Ibid*, file 9, f. 1v

44 *Ibid*. file 19, f. 2v

45 *Ibid*, file 19

46 *Ibid*, file 9, f. 1v

47 This journal was published in St. Petersburg from 1818 to 1884, with changing directions and editors. From 1818 to 1830 Svinin was its acting publisher.

48 *Son of the Fatherland*, 1817, No. 13, p. 56

49 *Severnaya Pchela* (Northern Bee), April 17, 1834

50 TsGIA, fund 472, inv. 13 (66), file 166, f. 1

51 *Ibid*, f. 2

52 *Svinin's Russian Museum: A Short Inventory of Objects*, St. Petersburg, 1829

53 Fortress on the River Yaik, today called the Ural River.

54 A. S. Pushkin, *Complete Works*, Moscow, 1949, v. 2, p. 112

CATALOGUE

Album in a brown leather binding with the
inscription: *Voyage aux E. U. de l'Amérique par
P. Sv. № 11*
Cover size: 10.7×16.7 cm
Page size: 10×16.3 cm
Size of pictures glued to album pages:
8.3×14.4 cm
Pictures framed in black (India ink).
All drawings executed in watercolor.
Received in 1953 from the Main Administration
for Matters of Art of the USSR Ministry
of Culture.

1. **Landscape with Buildings**
   p-49077

2. **Rapids**
   Inscribed in pencil on the back: No. 7.
   p-49078

3. **Rainbow**
   Inscribed in pencil on the back: No. 28.
   p-49079

4. **Landscape with Bridge**
   Inscribed in pencil on the back: No. 23.
   p-49080

5. **Landscape with Fishermen**
   Inscribed in pencil on the back: No. 12.
   p-49081

6. **Estate**
   Inscribed in pencil on the back: No. 57.
   p-49082

7. **Landscape with Moon**
   p-49083

8. **Mansion in a Park**
   p-49084

9. **Leveling a Road**
   Inscribed in pencil on the back: No. 9.
   p-49085

10. **View of a Settlement**
    Inscribed in pencil on the back: No. 26.
    p-49086

11. **In the Forest**
    Inscribed in pencil on the back: No. 8.
    p-49087

12. **On the Plantation**
    Inscribed in pencil on the back: No. 22.
    p-49088

13. **In a Ruined Mansion**
    Inscribed in pencil on the back: No. 10.
    p-49089

14. **Meeting of Two Boats**
    Inscribed in pencil on the back: No. 11.
    p-49090

15. **City on a River**
    Inscribed in pencil on the back: No. 60.
    p-49091

16. **View of a River**
    Inscribed in pencil on the back: No. 49.
    p-49092

17. **View of a City on a Riverbank**
    Inscribed in pencil on the back: No. 48.
    p-49093

18. **City on a Riverbank**
    Inscribed in pencil on the back: No. 78.
    p-49094

19. **Work on a Riverbank**
    Inscribed in pencil on the back: No. 14.
    p-49095

20. **Riverbanks**
    Inscribed in pencil on the back: No. 15.
    p-49096

21. **Bridge Across a River**
    Inscribed in pencil on the back: No. 69.
    p-49097

22. **View of a City on a River**
    Inscribed in pencil on the back: No. 70.
    p-49098

23. **Fort on a River**
    Inscribed in pencil on the back: No. 68.
    p-49099

24. **Building with a Tower**
    Inscribed in pencil on the back: No. 67.
    p-49100

25. **View of a City from a River**
    Inscribed in pencil on the back: No. 66.
    p-49101

26. **Landscape with River**
    Inscribed in pencil on the back: L it A.
    p-49102

27. **View of a City**
    Inscribed in pencil on the back: No. 65.
    p-49103

28. **View of Rocky Riverbanks**
    Inscribed in pencil on the back: No. 36.
    p-49104

29. **View of a River in the Mountains**
    Inscribed in pencil on the back: No. 35.
    p-49105

30. **Fort**
    Inscribed in pencil on the back: No. 50.
    p-49106

31. **Village by a River**

    Inscribed in pencil on the back: No. 33.
    p-49107

32. **Landscape with River**
    Inscribed in pencil on the back: No. 29.
    p-49108

33. **Landscape with a Road Along a Riverbank**

Inscribed in pencil on the back: No. 32.

p-49109

34. **Landscape with Road**

Inscribed in pencil on the back: No. 31.

p-49110

35. **View of a Village on a Riverbank**

Inscribed in pencil on the back: No. 30.

p-49111

36. **Town on a River**

Inscribed in pencil on the back: No. 53.

p-49112

37. **Landscape with River**

Inscribed in pencil on the back: No. 73.

p-49113

38. **Obverse and Reverse of a Medal in Honor of George Washington**

p-49114

39. **Mountain Road**

Inscribed in pencil on the back: No. 24.

p-49116

40. **View of an Island with Tall Trees**

Inscribed in pencil on the back: No. 16.

p-49117

Album in a brown leather binding with the inscription *П. П. Свиньин* [P. P. Svinin] written in gold letters on the cover.
Cover size: 27.8×35.4 cm
Page size: 27×33.6 cm

Size of pictures glued to album pages: 13.3×10.3 cm or 10.3×13.3 cm
Pictures framed in black (India ink).
All drawings executed in watercolor.
At the end of the album a few watercolors on Russian subjects are glued in. (These are not included in the edition.)
Received in 1953 from the Main Administration for Matters of Art of the USSR Ministry of Culture.

41. **Portrait of George Washington.**
From the original by Gilbert Stuart

p-49039

42. **Portrait of General Moreau**

p-49040

43. **Washington's Tomb at Mount Vernon**

Reproduced: 1930, No. 43* (General Washington's tomb at Mount Vernon. $7^3/_4 \times 5$)

p-49041

44. **View of Washington**

Reproduced: 1930, No. 42* (Washington and Georgetown from the road approaching Alexandria. $8^1/_8 \times 4^1/_2$)

p-49042

* The asterisk denotes the edition: *Picturesque United States of America 1811, 1812, 1813, being A Memoir on Paul Svinin, Russian diplomatic officer, artist and author, containing copious excerpts from his account of his travels in America, with Fifty-Two Reproductions of Water Colors in His Own Sketch-book.* By Avrahm Yarmolinsky. Introduction by R. T. H. Halsey, New York, 1930.

45. The Pennsylvania Academy of Fine
Arts (The First Art School in America)
Reproduced: 1930, No. 24* (The Pennsylvania Academy of Fine Arts, Philadelphia,
the first art school in America. $7^3/_4 \times 5^1/_2$)

p-49043

46. View of a Village from a River

p-49044

47. New Tall Building in New York
(New York City Hall)
Reproduced: 1930, No. 4* (The new City
Hall, New York, completed in 1811.
$9^1/_4 \times 6$)

p-49045

48. River with Rapids

p-49046

49. St. Paul's Cathedral in New York

p-49047

50. View of New York
Reproduced: 1930, No. 5* (New York City
and Harbor from Weehawken. $10^1/_8 \times 6$)

p-49048

51. Niagara Falls by Moonlight
Reproduced: P. P. Svinin, *An Attempt at
a Pictorial Account of a Trip Across North
America*, St. Petersburg, 1815, between
p. 155 and p. 168; 1930, No. 37* (Niagara
Falls, Table Rock, by moonlight. $9^3/_4 \times$
$\times 13^1/_4$)

p-49049

52. Niagara Falls from the Canadian Side
Reproduced: 1930, No. 38* (Niagara Falls,
Canadian Side by moonlight. $13^1/_2 \times 9^1/_4$)

p-49050

53. Waterfall
Inscribed in ink under the picture on the
album page: *Водопад на реке* [Waterfall
on a River]

p-49051

54. Niagara Falls

p-49052

55. Remains of a Beaver Dam near
Kenneber

p-49053

56. Indians in a Boat
Reproduced: 1930, No. 32* (A fanciful
sketch of the two Indians represented on
plates 29 and 30, and a white man, probably
our author. $8^5/_8 \times 5^7/_8$)

p-49054

57. New Bridge near Philadelphia
Reproduced: 1930, No. 25* (The covered
(Upper) bridge over the Schuylkill River in
Philadelphia; Lemon Hill in the back-
ground. $9^5/_8 \times 6^7/_8$)

p-49055

58. Landscape in the Vicinity of
Philadelphia

p-49056

59. **View of Morrisville, General Moreau's Country House in Pennsylvania**

Reproduced: P. P. Svinin, *An Attempt at a Pictorial Account of a Trip Across North America*, St. Petersburg, 1815, between p. 107 and p. 109; 1930, No. 33* (General Moreau's country house at Morrisville, Pennsylvania. $7^5/_8 \times 5^3/_8$)

p-49057

60. **Worship Service of Negro Methodists**

Reproduced: P. P. Svinin, *An Attempt at a Pictorial Account of a Trip Across North America*, St. Petersburg, 1815, p. 43; 1930, No. 18* (Frenzied Negro Methodists holding a religious meeting in a Philadelphia alley. $9^7/_8 \times 8^1/_2$)

p-49058

61. **View of Richmond**

p-49059

62. **Hamilton's Obelisk at Weehawken**

Reproduced: 1930, No. 6* (The monument to Alexander Hamilton erected on the spot where he fell in his duel with Aaron Burr at Weehawken. $7^5/_8 \times 5^3/_8$)

p-49060

63. **Baptism**

Reproduced: 1930, No. 19* (A Philadelphia Anabaptist submersion during a thunderstorm. $9^3/_4 \times 7$)

p-49061

64. **American Stagecoach**

Reproduced: 1930, No 11* (Travel by stagecoach near Trenton, New Jersey. $9^3/_4 \times 6^7/_8$)

p-49062

65. **Codfishing**

Reproduced: P. P. Svinin, *An Attempt at a Pictorial Account of a Trip Across North America*, St. Petersburg, 1815, p. 205; 1930, No. 1* (Replenishing the ship's larder with codfish off the banks of Newfoundland. $8^5/_8 \times 5^7/_8$)

p-49063

66. **Indian Antiquities**

Reproduced: 1930, No. 31* (Indian antiquities: a frog-shaped cup and two vases — apparently a copy of a magazine illustration. $8^1/_4 \times 6$)

p-49064

67. **Moravian Sisters**

Reproduced: 1930, No. 26* (Moravian Sisters. 8×6)

p-49065

68. **City Street**

Size of picture: 7×4.2 cm
Etchings from P. P. Svinin's book *An Attempt at a Pictorial Account of a Trip Across North America* (St. Petersburg, 1815), the originals are not included in the albums belonging to the Russian Museum collection.

p-49066

INFORMATION ABOUT THE WRITERS, ARTISTS, AND PUBLIC FIGURES MENTIONED IN THE TEXT

Adams, John Quincy (1767—1848), American statesman and diplomat. First U.S. envoy to Russia (1809—14), U.S. envoy to England (1815—17), U.S. Secretary of State (1817—25), U.S. President (1825—29).

Alexander I (Alexander Pavlovich, 1777—1825), Russian Emperor from 1801 to 1825.

Arakcheyev, Alexei Andreyevich (1769—1834), Count, Minister of War, Chairman of the War Department of the State Council. An influential figure during the reign of Alexander I, he was not popular among the Russian intelligentsia.

Briullov, Karl Pavlovich (1799—1852), great Russian artist. Painted the famous picture *The Last Day of Pompeii* (Russian Museum, St. Petersburg) and many portraits.

Dashkov, Andrei Yakovlevich (?—1831), statesman, diplomat. In 1808 appointed Consul General to the North American United States. In 1811 appointed Envoy Extraordinary and Minister Plenipotentiary. In 1820 appo-inted to a mission in Constantinople where he headed the Commercial Office. From 1821 he lived in Russia.

Elizaveta Alexeyevna, born Princess Louise-Maria-Augusta (1779—1826), Empress, wife of Alexander I.

Gogol, Nikolai Vasilyevich (1809—1852), great Russian writer.

Ivanov, Alexander Andreyevich (1806—1858), outstanding Russian artist. From 1830 lived in Italy, where he painted his famous work *The Appearance of Christ to the People* (Tretyakov Gallery, Moscow).

Izmailov, Alexander Yefimovich (1779—1831), poet, fable writer, journalist, publisher of the *Blagonamerenny* (*Loyal*) journal which came out in St. Petersburg from 1818 to 1826.

Khrapovitsky, Alexander Vasilyevich (1749—1801), statesman, one of the secretaries of Catherine the Great, writer, poet.

190

Kiprensky, Orest Adamovich (1782—1836), artist. Painted numerous portraits of his contemporaries.

Korneyev, Yemelyan Mikhailovich (1780—after 1839). Studied history painting at the St. Petersburg Academy of Arts, traveled extensively across Russia. His album of costume sketches is extant and can be viewed in the Russian Museum in St. Petersburg.

Kozlov, N. Ya. In August 1811 appointed Consul General in Philadelphia.

Levitsky, Dmitry Grigoryevich (1735—1822), artist, portraitist.

Lieven, Khristofor Andreyevich (1774—1838), Russian envoy to London.

Lomonosov, Mikhail Vasilyevich (1711—1765), famous scientist, poet, artist, inventor.

Longinov, Nikolai Mikhailovich (1779—1853), secretary to the Empress Elizaveta Alexeyevna.

Losenko, Anton Pavlovich (1737—1773), artist, one of the first Russian instructors at the St Petersburg Academy of Arts.

Martynov, Andrei Yefimovich (1768—1826), landscape artist. Studied at the St.-Petersburg Academy of Arts from 1773 to 1788, after that he received a scholarship to continue his training in Italy. He was among the envoys of the Russian Embassy who traveled to Peking in 1804. Martynov painted numerous views of Siberia and China. Traveled extensively in the Crimea and Caucasus.

Moreau, Jean Victor (1763—1813), French military leader, general. At first a supporter of Napoleon, was accused of conspiracy and arrested in 1804. After being pardoned, emigrated to the United States. In 1813 was mortally wounded by the French near Dresden while on his way to Russia.

Nicholas I (Nikolai Pavlovich, 1796—1855), Russian Emperor from 1825.

Peter the Great (Pyotr Alexeyevich, 1672—1725), Russian Tsar from 1682. Founder of St. Petersburg. Reformer.

Petrov, Vasily Petrovich (1770—1811), landscape artist. Studied at the St. Petersburg Academy of Arts. He was dispatched to Siberia as Artist for the Department of Mountain and Mineral Surveys. Created many paintings and graphic works with views of Siberia.

Pugachev, Yemelyan Ivanovich (c. 1742—1775), a Don cossack. Led the Peasant Rebellion of 1773—75. Executed.

Pushchin, Pavel Sergeyevich (1789—1869), officer. Took part in battles against Napoleon's army. Author of *Diaries* with detailed descriptions of the military campaigns of 1812—14.

Pushkin, Alexander Sergeyevich (1799—1837), great Russian poet.

Sinyavin, Dmitry Nikolayevich (1763—1831), military leader and statesman.

Tropinin, Vasily Andreyevich (1776—1857), artist. Painted numerous portraits of his contemporaries.

Turgenev, Alexander Ivanovich (1784—1845), man of letters, archeologist, public figure.

Turgenev, Nikolai Ivanovich (1789—1871), brother of Alexander Turgenev. One of the leaders who prepared the Decembrist Rebellion on December 14, 1825. From 1824 lived abroad. Given the death sentence in his absence.

Venetsianov, Alexei Gavrilovich (1780—1847), founder of Russian genre painting. Opened a school in which he taught students his own method, which was noticeably different from that used at the Academy of Arts.

Vyazemsky, Pyotr Andreyevich (1792—1878), Prince, poet, journalist, literary critic.

Volkonsky, Pyotr Mikhailovich (1776—1852), Prince, Adjutant-General, head of the General Staff, Minister of the Imperial Court. From 1850 Field Marshal.

Vorontsov, Alexander Romanovich (1741—1805), statesman, diplomat.

Zhukovsky, Vasily Andreyevich (1783—1852), poet, one of Pushkin's closest friends, tutor of Emperor Nicholas I.